Mel Bay's

Fun with the

OCARINA

2 3 4 5 6 7 8 9 0

Fingering

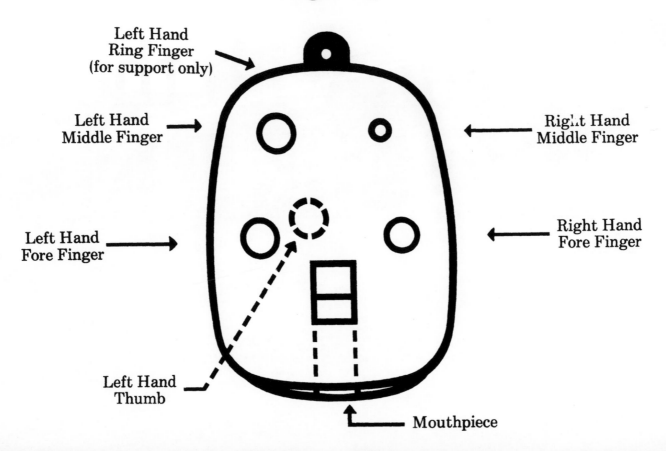

Playing Instructions

To play the ocarina, rest the mouthpiece on your lips with the body of the instrument slanting downward at approximately a 45° angle. The thumb is under the instrument and over the round hole in the back called the "thumb hole." The forefinger and middle finger of each hand cover the two holes on each side. The instrument should be held gently in the lips and placed not too far into the mouth.

To tongue the instrument, gently make the syllable "du - du" or "tu - tu."

The pitch of the instrument will vary according to the angle at which you are holding the instrument. Therefore, it is important to hold the instrument steady and to practice utilizing long tones to develop clarity of sound.

Fingering Chart

For 4 and 5 Hole Ocarinas

● = closed tone hole
○ = open tone hole or thumb hole
⊗ = closed thumb hole

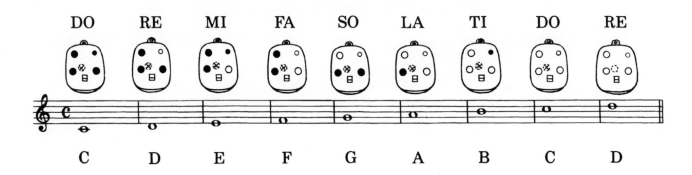

Contents

Types Of Notes

o ♩ ♩· ♩ ♩· ♪ ♪	THE TYPE OF NOTE WILL INDICATE THE LENGTH OF ITS SOUND.

o	THIS IS A WHOLE NOTE.	o	= 4 BEATS A WHOLE - NOTE WILL RECEIVE FOUR BEATS OR COUNTS.
♩	THIS IS A HALF NOTE.	♩	= 2 BEATS A HALF - NOTE WILL RECEIVE TWO BEATS OR COUNTS.
♩·	DOTTED HALF NOTE	♩·	= 3 COUNTS
♩	THIS IS A QUARTER NOTE.	♩	= 1 BEAT A QUARTER NOTE WILL RECEIVE ONE BEAT OR COUNT.
♩·	DOTTED QUARTER NOTE.	♩·	= 1½ COUNTS
♪	THIS IS AN EIGHTH NOTE	♪	= ½ BEAT AN EIGHTH - NOTE WILL RECEIVE ONE - HALF BEAT OR COUNT. (2 FOR 1 BEAT)
♪	THIS IS A SIXTEENTH NOTE.	♪	= ¼ BEAT - 4 PER BEAT

Rests

A REST is a sign to designate a period of silence. This period of silence will be of the same duration as the note to which it corresponds.

   7   THIS IS AN EIGHTH REST   **{** THIS IS A QUARTER REST

   7̇   THIS IS A SIXTEENTH REST

   —   THIS IS A HALF REST
          Note that it lays on the line.
   —   THIS IS A WHOLE REST
          Note that it hangs down from the line.

NOTES

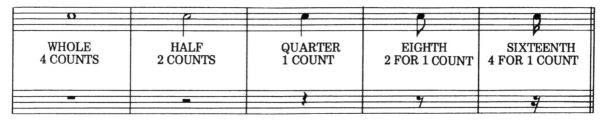

| WHOLE 4 COUNTS | HALF 2 COUNTS | QUARTER 1 COUNT | EIGHTH 2 FOR 1 COUNT | SIXTEENTH 4 FOR 1 COUNT |

RESTS

The Time Signature

The above examples are the common types of time signatures to be used in this book.

 The top number indicates the number of beats per measure
The bottom number indicates the type of note receiving one beat per measure

 beats per measure

a quarter - note receives one beat.

BEATS PER MEASURE

EACH EIGHTH - NOTE
RECEIVES ONE FULL
BEAT

 Signifies so called "common time" and is simply another way of designating 4/4 time.

Notes Used

= closed tone hole
= open tone hole or thumb hole
= closed thumb hole

C   D   E   F   G

Au Clair De La Lune

Accompaniment Chords:

Lightly Row

Accompaniment Chords:

Notes Used

● = closed tone hole
○ = open tone hole or thumb hole
⊗ = closed thumb hole

C   D   E   F   G

Accompaniment
Chords:

Oh When The Saints

C | Hold for value of both notes. |

Notes Used

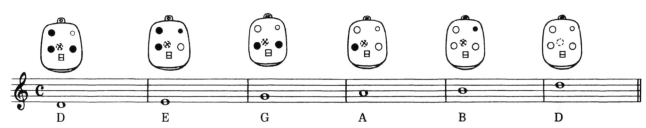

D   E   G   A   B   D

Accompaniment
Chords:

Ol' Dan Tucker

Notes Used

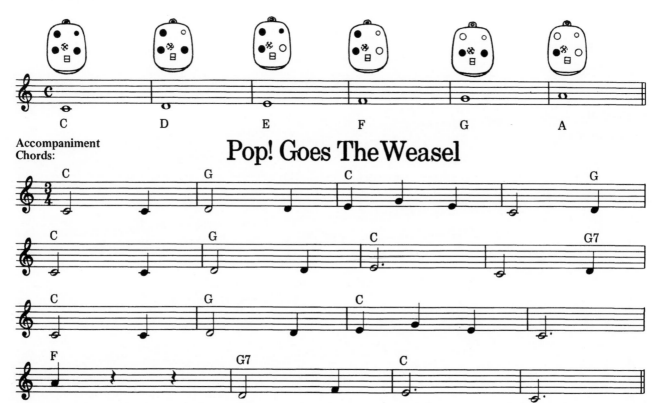

Notes Used

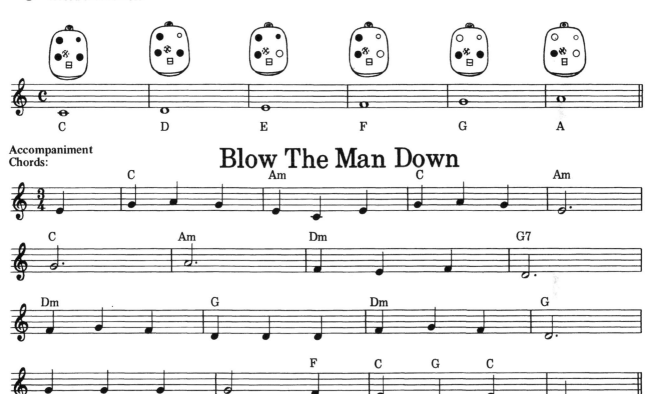

Notes Used

● = closed tone hole
○ = open tone hole or thumb hole
⊗ = closed thumb hole

C D E F G A

Accompaniment Chords:

This Little Light Of Mine

Notes Used

● = closed tone hole
○ = open tone hole or thumb hole
⊗ = closed thumb hole

C   D   E   F   G   A

Kum Ba Ya

Accompaniment Chords:

Notes Used

● = closed tone hole
○ = open tone hole or thumb hole
⊗ = closed thumb hole

Liza Jane

Accompaniment Chords:

Notes Used

● = closed tone hole
○ = open tone hole or thumb hole
⊗ = closed thumb hole

C   D   E   G   A   B   C

Accompaniment
Chords:

Goin' Home

Dvorak

Notes Used

● = closed tone hole
○ = open tone hole or thumb hole
⊗ = closed thumb hole

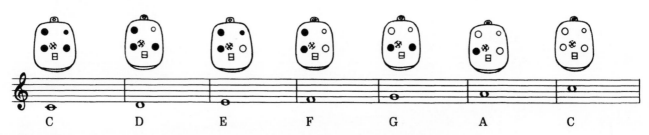

C   D   E   F   G   A   C

She Wore A Yellow Ribbon

Accompaniment Chords:

Notes Used

= closed tone hole
= open tone hole or thumb hole
= closed thumb hole

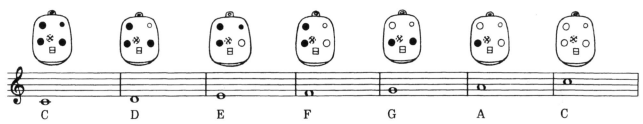

C D E F G A C

Jacob's Ladder

Notes Used

● = closed tone hole
○ = open tone hole or thumb hole
⊗ = closed thumb hole

Lolly Too Dum

Accompaniment Chords:

Notes Used

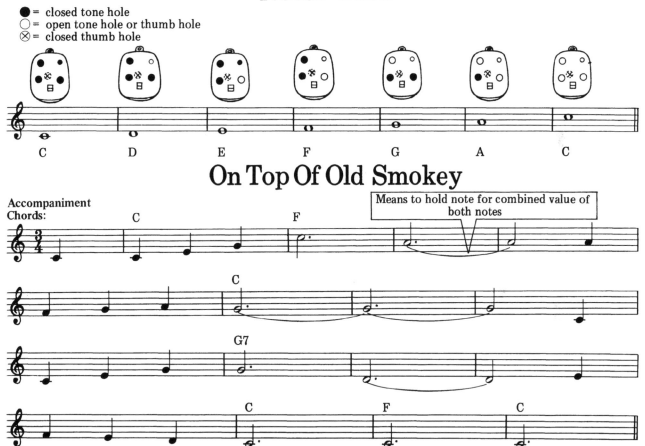

● = closed tone hole
○ = open tone hole or thumb hole
⊗ = closed thumb hole

C   D   E   F   G   A   C

On Top Of Old Smokey

Accompaniment
Chords:

Means to hold note for combined value of both notes

Notes Used

● = closed tone hole
○ = open tone hole or thumb hole
⊗ = closed thumb hole

C D E F G A C

Rise & Shine

Accompaniment Chords:

Notes Used

C D E F G A B C

Song From The Magic Flute

Accompaniment
Chords:

Mozart

Go back to number ① and play to end of song

Notes Used

● = closed tone hole
○ = open tone hole or thumb hole
⊗ = closed thumb hole

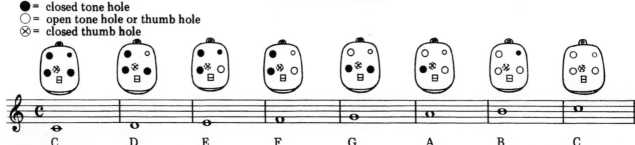

C D E F G A B C

Believe Me If All Those Endearing Young Charms

Accompaniment
Chords:

Notes Used

● = closed tone hole
○ = open tone hole or thumb hole
⊗ = closed thumb hole

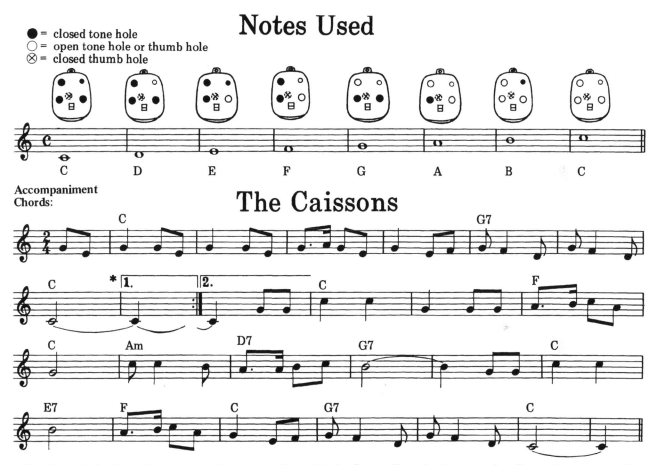

C   D   E   F   G   A   B   C

Accompaniment Chords:

The Caissons

Notes Used

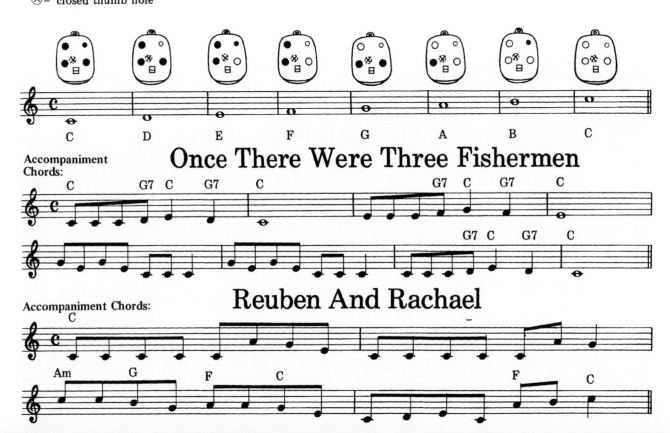

● = closed tone hole
○ = open tone hole or thumb hole
⊗ = closed thumb hole

C D E F G A B C

Accompaniment Chords:

Once There Were Three Fishermen

C   G7 C   G7   C   G7 C   G7   C

G7 C   G7   C

Accompaniment Chords:

Reuben And Rachael

C

Am   G   F   C   F   C

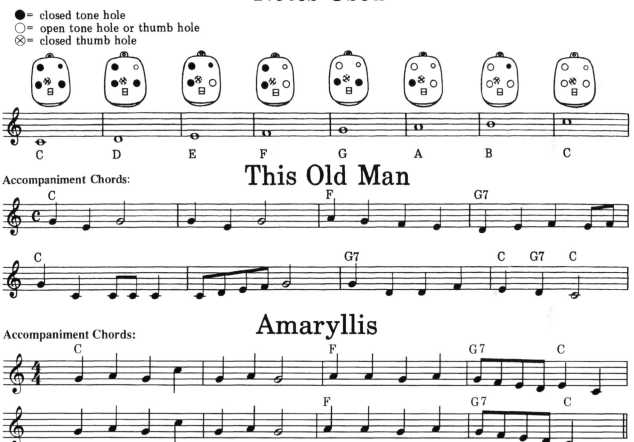

Notes Used

● = closed tone hole
○ = open tone hole or thumb hole
⊗ = closed thumb hole

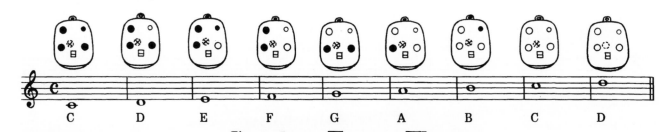

Stephen Foster Theme

Accompaniment Chords:

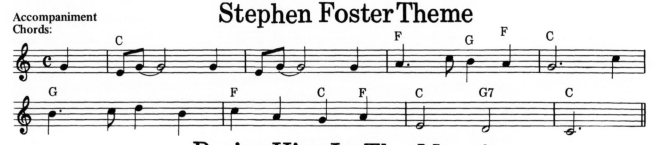

Praise Him In The Morning

Accompaniment Chords:

Notes Used

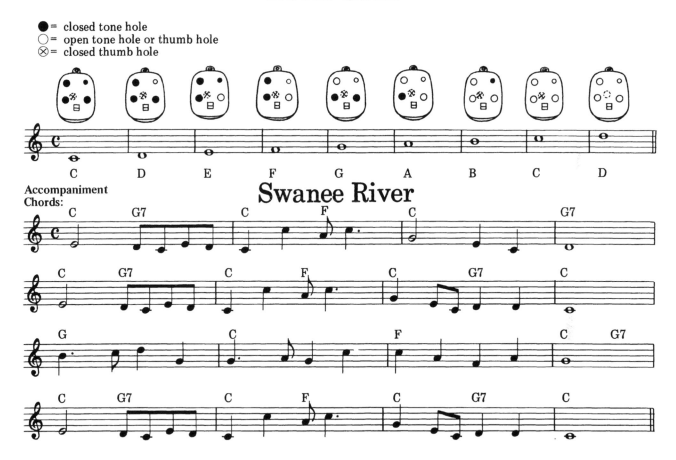

● = closed tone hole
○ = open tone hole or thumb hole
⊗ = closed thumb hole

C D E F G A B C D

Swanee River

Accompaniment Chords: